Community Helpers Series

New House, New Town

ANNE NEIGOFF

Pictures: Lois Axeman

Albert Whitman & Company

Picture Dictionary

architect

bricklayer

bulldozer man

carpenter

cement worker

electrician

Copyright ©1973 by
Albert Whitman & Company, Chicago
Published simultaneously in Canada
by George J. McLeod, Limited,
Toronto
Printed in the U.S.A.

Library of Congress Cataloging in Publication Data
Neigoff, Anne, 1911-
    New house, new town.

    (Community helpers series)
    SUMMARY: A family arranges to have a house
built in a new town.
    1. House construction—Juvenile literature.
[1. House construction] I. Axeman, Lois, illus.
II. Title.
TH4811.N36   690'.8'64   72-13352
ISBN 0-8075-5570-3

movers

painter

paperhanger

plumber

surveyor

telephone man

Tony Kim calls out, "Stop, Amy!" and
Tim asks, "Mom, does Amy have
to play here?"
Mother looks at Dad.
Dad picks Amy up.
He says, "We need more room.
We need room for work and play and sleep."
"Yes," Mother says. "Our family needs
a new home."

What kind of home do the Kims need?
A big house, a little house, a trailer house
on wheels?
Mother and Dad talk about houses for rent
and houses for sale.
"Let's buy a new home," Mother says.
"There's a new town near here," Dad says.
"Let's look at houses there."

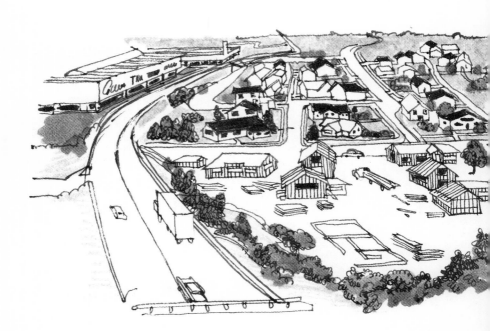

So off to New Town go Mother and Dad,
Tim and Tony and little Amy.
"Once this was farm land," Dad says.
"And now it's a town," Mother says.
"Look at the streets and stores."
"I see the school," Tony says.
"And a park," says Tim.
"There are places to work," Dad says.
"I see a factory and office buildings."

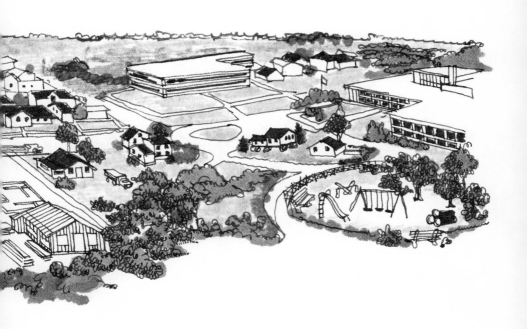

Many towns just grow with a street here
and a street there.
But New Town was planned to be
a good place to live.
It has homes to rent and homes to buy.
The Kims stop at an office.
"Hello," says Mrs. Rio. "I work
for New Town Homes. Let me help you."

"We want to buy a house," say the Kims.
"The house must be big enough.
It must have safe places to play.
It must not cost too much."
Mrs. Rio says, "Let's see the model houses.
Then I'll show you a lot."
"What's a lot?" asks Tim.
"It's the land where your house
will be built," Mrs. Rio tells Tim.

The model houses look ready to live in.
The Kims see a house for two families.
They see a house with one floor.
They see a house with two floors.
Mother says, "Here's a room for Amy.
But the closet is too small."
"We can build a bigger closet," says Mrs. Rio.
"This can be our room," say Tony and Tim.

Then Mrs. Rio and the Kims look at lots.
"I like this lot," Mother says. "It's near
the school and near stores, too."
Dad says, "I like this street.
The streetlights are already here."
"Look at the men working," says Tony.
Mrs. Rio says, "They are surveyors.
They mark just how big a lot is."
"Maybe boys will live there," says Tim.

The Kims go back to the New Town office.
They look at the plans for the house
they liked best.
An architect drew the plans.
Mrs. Rio tells what the house will cost.
"Thank you," say Dad and Mother.
"We will think about this and call you."
Tim and Tony already know what they want.
"Let's live here," they say. "It's great."

The Kims look at some other houses.
But they like the house in New Town best.
It is the house they want for a home.
"Can we help build it?" ask the boys.
Dad laughs and shakes his head.
"It takes many workers to build a house.
The contractor for New Town Homes will
get the workers for us.
We will go see him now."

The contractor says, "I have carpenters, cement workers, plumbers, painters, and other workers ready.
They will begin building your house."
"Can we help?" Tim and Tony ask.
"It will be your turn to help when you move in," laughs the contractor.

Long ago when our country was new,
a family could build its own home.
The men and boys cut down trees.
They shaped the logs for the walls.
They split shingles for the roof.
Sometimes neighbors came to help.
Then there was a house-raising party.
What a good time!

The Kims won't have a log house.
But their frame house will be built of wood.
The contractor uses the architect's plans.
He orders everything he needs for building.
A man with a bulldozer comes.
In the empty lot he digs a hole where
the surveyors put markers.

A house does not just stand on the ground.
It needs strong walls, or footings, to
hold it up.
Workmen build wooden forms in the hole
made by the bulldozer.
They pour wet cement between the forms.
When the cement is hard, the workmen
take away the wooden forms.
Now it's time for the carpenters.

Here comes a load of lumber.
Carpenters fit heavy boards along
the footings.
Next they build a floor for the house.
Now Tony and Tim can't see the basement.
Up go strong posts called studs.
Soon the house frame is up.
It looks like a peek-a-boo house to Amy.

Long wooden rafters go up for the roof.
Bang! Bang! The carpenters nail on
plywood sheets to close in the house.
They leave holes for doors and windows.
The house looks like a big wooden box.

Now in go the windows and doors.
The carpenters cover the plywood
with special paper to keep out the rain.
They nail on siding.
Paper covers the roof, too.
Over the paper go shingles that won't burn.
A bricklayer comes to build the chimney.

Other workers are busy, too.
The plumber puts in pipes for water
and pipes for heating.
The electrician puts in wires for
electric lights and a washing machine
and everything that needs electricity.

Now men line the house walls on the inside
to keep the Kims warm in winter and
cool in summer.
Wallboard goes up on the walls.
It hides the pipes and wires and studs.

"Is our house ready?" ask Tony and Tim.
No — there are tile floors to put in.
Workers must finish the kitchen and
bathroom, the cupboards and closets.
The painters come, and a paperhanger puts
pink paper in Amy's room.

Tony says, "How long building takes!"
"I wish it could be quick," says Tim.
"Some houses are built in just a day
or two," Dad says.
"I'll show you one."

Tim and Tony watch men unload parts
of a new house from a big truck.
Each part was made at a factory.
Even the pipes and wires are put in.
The parts fit together like a puzzle.
How fast this house goes up on its footings!
Dad says, "This is a prefab house.
It's one way to build a house fast."

Now the house for the Kims is almost ready.
The stove, the refrigerator, the sink go in.
The furnace, the washer and dryer are in.
The telephone man comes.

A cement walk goes to the front door.
There's a driveway for the car, too.
The yard around the house is smooth
and ready for grass.
"We'll plant flowers and some little trees,"
Dad tells the boys. "You can help."

At last their new house in the new town
is ready for the Kims.
Here come the movers.
Beds and chairs and tables,
pictures and clothes and books go in.
Tony and Tim carry their model planes.
Amy brings her bear.
Hello, new house!
The Kim family is moving in.

Many workers built the new house.
Many workers are building New Town.
There are many kinds of houses.
Each house is right for some family.
"Our new house is home now," Tim says.
"So is New Town," says Tony.
Good night, new house in New Town!